The Art of Grilling

Byron Hoot, 2020

hootnhowlpoetry.com

The Art of Grilling, Religious Reflections was written over a series of weeks while grilling dinner. The grill was under the deck against an outside wall facing west. Which means it was protected from the prevailing winds. And so was I. And so I cooked. Drank an IPA and read Rilke's *Book of Hours*. Then found myself writing poems in response to his. On the pages of the edition I was reading.

Outside of the first poem, the poems correspond to Rilke's. I suppose it could be seen as a liturgical exercise – his poems answered by mine.

Fortunately, there are no wrong responses. Unfortunately, the responses are not as good as Rilke's poems. But my name is Hoot not Rilke. His poems spoke, speak to me and at that time I was moved to respond. To the best of my ability.

I am a son of a preacher. Actually, generations of preachers. And while I am more than deeply suspicious of religious institutions, I believe in the urge – inherent – towards religious experience as a significant part of my life that makes its essence essential for a richer, fuller, and more courageous life.

I often turned the flame lower so I could stay out longer sitting in the chair that stayed out all year, reading a poem, sipping an IPA, and writing what would not let me alone.

I hope you enjoy these poems.

— Byron Hoot

I Cook Outside In Winter	6
Touch	8
As If	9
All Graven Images Are Idols	10
Being Who We Are	11
Out of the Darkness	12
Always Someone	13
Make No Mistake	14
Tired of Thinking	16
Somewhere Deep Inside	17
We Do Much to Others	18
There Is Something Deeply Known	19
The Only Way to Praise God	20
What Is There In Me to Match You?	22
If I Desire Less	23
Our Urge to Build	25
When You Breathed Into Us	26
If You Are	27
Words and Images Fail	28
Who Dreams Whom to Wakefulness?	29
This Image of God	30
Finding You Everywhere	31
It's True	32
Make No Mistake	33
I Don't Understand Greatness	34
When I Ask, "Whom Do I Serve?"	36
Fear Not and Know	38
All the Stories Are Inside	39
What We Long For	40
I Am Is Hidden Always	42
Time Began With the Presence	44
Your Presence Is Never	45
The One Who Works Against You	47

Wherever I Go, There's God	48
Whatever I Do When the Heart	50
I Have Learned and Still Am Taught	51
After You Repeat After Me	52
So Many Things Have Been	53
We Are Born With the Voice of God	54
I Have Given You Metaphor	55
Before Any Scripture Written	56
No Mistake	57
I Am What You Are Not	59
I Am Not Afraid Of the Dark	60
So I See You	62
How I Have Known You	64
The Drama of Our Lives	65
Once Jacob, At Five Said	67
What We Take In We Put Back	68
You Are the Shape-shifter	69
It Is Difficult	70
The First Falsehood	72
I Am Asked	74
Where Our Freedom Lies	75
In This Generation or the Next	77
Who and What We	78
All Has Been Lost	79
And When We Come Again	80
We Are Not Weak	81
This Quest Goes On, Is Handed Off	82
Always For	83
There Is No Denying How Far Away	84
"My Help Cometh from the Hills"	86
You Cannot Find God in Cities	87
If We Cannot Pray	88
Deepest Desire	89

Our Greatest Fear 90
The Proclamation of Who I Am 91
I Want To Hear Your Voice 92
What Is True Is How I Can Be 93
And The Seduction of What 94
The Wealth That Matters 95
We Who Lack the Riches of the World 97
When You Have Given Up the Quest 98
Everywhere You Step 99
The Voice of God Is Like the Wind 100
The Trees Know Nothing of the Laws 101
Yes 102
It Has Taken Me a Long Time 103

I Cook Outside In Winter

I cook outside in winter,

Spring, summer, fall.

Longer in winter. . . I stay

Outside;

    The fire and the cold

Neutralized,

        At least for

As long as the grill

Heats enough to cook

The meat.

    I like the winter

Most of all;

    It leaves me outside

Longer to see and hear,

To smell and taste,

To touch what

Lingers at twilight,

Twilight where what is not

Seen in day

    Appears.

Touch

To touch

To taste

To feel

To hear

      All caught in five words:

I am that I am,

And everything is

As we too are born turning

And hearing another say,

I am that I am.

As If

It dawns on me:

To say I am that I am

Has no boundaries,

No persona,

No projection

Just that eternal

Fact of being

Here and now

In eternity

That scoffs at the names of things

As if they mean anything.

All Graven Images Are Idols

All graven images are idols,

Especially the ones made

From words

Where form and beauty are always

Grammatically correct.

The one I pray

To is never fully seen,

Knows everything cannot be revealed

And so demands a lover's trust

For one more minute of eternity

Here now, there now,

Always now in darkness and in light

Whispering sweet nothings in my ear.

Being Who We Are

In the realm of being whom we are,

Which is everywhere among us,

It takes two to know who we are

Like root and branches,

Sun and moon,

Winter and summer,

Man and woman,

You and I

One singing, I am;

One singing, Who are you?

The song done in perfect harmony,

Dancing along the way

Singing all the time.

Out of the Darkness

I was born out of the darkness

And still love that darkness

That holds everything I am

And I am to be:

There, all understanding is understood

Wordlessly.

What happens and what and who

I embrace are not always

Known by me at the moment

But eventually –

All joys.

All sorrows,

All dreams,

All nightmares,

All of my life lovingly.

Always Someone
There is always someone else wanting

To be us when we need to be whom

We are.

When it's

The God who says, I am that I am

We're not far from being

I am too.

That essence we need is always

Close, closer, right inside

But often we don't ask,

Who are you?

And wait for the reply –

I am you,

You are me;

Now, God says,

Repeat after Me.

Make No Mistake

Make no mistake:

There are a thousand and one

Distractions,

If not paid attention

To with the fullness they need,

Will debilitate you.

They don't demand much

Just the same type of attention

The big questions get.

Remember:

"Look under a stick

And I am there."

Remember:

Look under a stick

And you are there

The two making a third

And the distraction full

Of satisfaction needed

And so

    Blesses everything you do.

Tired of Thinking

I am tired of thinking

Of a future financially sound.

My soul cringes

Knowing,

But not quite yet able to convince me,

That if I follow my destiny –

A fact still intact –

Everything

Will be provided that needs to be!

The question is:

What is destiny?

I hesitate before that door.

Somewhere Deep Inside

Somewhere deep inside

We carry that first

Killing of one brother

By another,

One sister

By another.

There are, how can

This be explained,

Parts of us

Who enrage each other

And rather than sacrificing

One for another

We kill and are haunted

By those last sighs

Until, if redeemed,

Some resurrection occurs

And we are whole again.

We Do Much to Others

We do much to others

We would not do to ourselves.

We put up with what others do

We would not permit ourselves to do.

We stand accused and accuser,

Christ and Judas,

Hope and despair

Moving prayerfully into compassion

Because every me is every you.

There Is Something Deeply Known

There is something deeply known

When we sing "*O Holy Night.*"

Something about

Where such a birth occurs,

Something about that third

Born from two,

Something about those wise men

And their long-lost brother shepherds

Who witness the night glory

Of birth and birth and birth

All the way to crucifixion

And birth again

After three nights

Just to be able to walk

With ourselves as we are

How can night be shunned at all?

And so we sing, "*O Holy Night.*"

The Only Way to Praise God

The only way to praise God

Is to be free

Of those selves

In me who hold me back.

It may take years to discern

Whose who –

        No matter.

To be able to be who

I am and am to be for just one moment

Is more eternity

Than many are given.

If I can do that longer,

What need for paradise

Beyond where here and now will be free, full

And I can praise God

As God praises me

Humming,

I am

Together again.

What Is There In Me to Match You?

What is there in me to match You?

Everything, I say, neither proud

Nor humble

      But grounded in the knowledge

To even conceive of one like You,

One like me

Something has to be there

For some metaphorical understanding

To occur.

If we were made in Your

Likeness and image,

There is no hubris to know

That You are me

And I am You

And we are

I am;

Of course, how that I am

Works itself out is what the stories are all about.

If I Desire Less

If I desire less

Than what is desirous for me,

How can I live?

I do not want

To be all to everyone,

Only all to myself

That will let me be

A disciple with

Those like me –

Those who are all they

Are to be.

Sounds easy; isn't –

I know:

But who else

Is there to be?

Let me clear the debris

And flow as that stream has

Always meant to:

Freely, deeply, reflecting,

Constantly moving, changing

And constantly

Always the same.

Our Urge to Build

Our urge to build

Sanctuary is our fear

Of seeing You as You

That admits that we can be

Who we are too.

The crumbling of what we build,

The way ideas and images fray

Into ghosts says it all

Unable to hide

Until, like You, we are found

Everywhere we are.

When You Breathed Into Us

When You breathed into us,

You knew we would want

That kiss again.

That exchange of breath,

Of lips against lips.

That's why to some You are

He, others You are She.

When the taste of such dreams

Becomes real by only a sliver,

It is enough to keep us

Seeking You all our lives

Whether we say we are or not.

If You Are

If you are a man,

A woman someone waits

To make you whole

Because we are not

Born whole

But with a longing for wholeness.

That one may be flesh and blood

May be in, and only in,

The realm of soul.

It doesn't matter;

We are not born complete

And so seek that one who

Seeks us

      Mutually being

Who the other needs.

It's been that way forever –

We are not enough

          Alone.

Words and Images Fail

Words and images fail;

The spoken word,

The painted form

          Are nothing

When Presence is everything.

What is true for God

Is true for us.

     We, like God, are

Beyond description,

Beyond capture

Though we, because we are who we are,

Are caught by both.

We have nothing else,

Except our presences

That wait for us to recognize

Them for who they are –

          As soon as

We see through the eyes of God.

Who Dreams Whom to Wakefulness?
Who dreams whom to wakefulness?

God dreams, man is;

Man dreams, God appears.

And all our longing,

From each one,

Is to be in the presence

Of the other

The way a man and woman

Come together to make one

And still remain who they are.

That is how God comes to me

And how I come to God

So dream

And wakefulness eternally.

This Image of God

This image of God

As father is too small;

And this image of me

Separated from God

Is not as it is

Though through

Our thinking we have minted

It to our souls

While the obvious goes unstated,

Unnoticed.

I reach for God

As God reaches for me:

The basic fact of the soul

Is reciprocity–

I get what I give

Bountifully.

Finding You Everywhere

Finding You everywhere so I

Find myself

      Wherever

You appear. Your invitation is,

"Here. Come here."

        And I come

Knowing there is something more

Of You to know,

Something more of me to find,

In pain or pleasure,

Hope or despair. . .

Wherever You are,

If I want to be,

I'll be there.

It's True
It's true:

    We all desire

To die, to be torn apart,

To be crucified

        But only if

We come back alive,

Whole in some different

Configuration where

We combine all ourselves

Into one seamless robe

Covering, revealing,

Warming, cooling

Everyone, everything.

Forget the thoughts of living forever

Unless you mean here and now.

Make No Mistake

Make no mistake: Who we are

Does not happen over night;

It may start with a sudden illumination

But it has to go beyond that

Into muscle bulging darkness

Where we wrestle against everyone –

All of us, all of God –

                And survive.

There's a path into and through and out of

That darkness

That lets us arrive in

The presence of who we are

Saying the only words

From which all else flows,

"I am. . . . "

I Don't Understand Greatness

I don't understand

Greatness

    Nor those who speak

Of God being far away.

I can barely grasp

What it means to be completely,

Wholly who and where I am

Let alone a word like great.

It's true: The language God

Speaks is not always spoken

And if it is caught by the ear

It sounds more like

Baby talk – ah, ooh.

Still, wherever I look

I get that sense God

Has just disappeared

And left some form of beauty for my

Eye that my heart knows

As I try to be

Wholly who and where I am

The hardest, easiest thing to do.

When I Ask, "Whom Do I Serve?"

When I ask, "Whom do I serve?"

And act in service to that

One in and beyond me

Things happen I can't explain.

Small things that layer up

In story, some I can tell,

Some I can't but feel

Them deep inside

Coming out in the best words

For the moment,

In acts that are asking to be done,

In seeing and touching,

In hearing, tasting, smelling

And the wonderful inability

To say just what I feel

In any way other than being

Who I am by serving

That one in and beyond

Inarticulate and clear

Always ready to call me by name.

Fear Not and Know

Fear not and know I am your God.

Fall,

Break,

Betray

Pretend you do not know Me –

It doesn't matter:

We both know everything does, if you will,

Draw us together.

You hide and I seek,

I hide and you seek.

We find ourselves in each other:

I've never pretended otherwise.

All the Stories Are Inside

All the stories are inside me:

I am King, Queen,

Husband, wife.

The older brother, the Prodigal.

All flow to and through and in

Me to create not mirrored images

Of themselves or others

But me, who I am to be,

Complete, whole with all the

Light and dark parts of me

Sitting down at table

A slight smile with eyes and mouth

Welcoming everyone,

Listening to the stories.

What We Long For

What we long for is complete;

It can never not be felt

In anything we do.

When we are breathed

Into by that longing

We start to live

As those who know

There is nothing that

Comes to them that is not

Theirs:

    Desire, fear,

        Pain, pleasure –

Everything is filled

With that divine longing

That sets us on fire

Pentecostal burning

Burning with complete

Unabashed desirous

Longing whose only prayer is,

I am that I am

Answered everywhere,

Yes, of course, you, too.

I Am Is Hidden Always

I am

    Is hidden always,

But not completely

Just beyond that meaning

Almost right,

    Just in the shadow

Of the curve of that hip,

That lift of the breast.

This is what lures

Us beyond who we

Are only willing to say

We are –

    That hint

Of that something almost

Within reach:

    Substantial,

Metaphorical fact,

Divine breathe breathed

Into us

        Until we can't

Recognize who we were,

Who we are so rapturously beautiful

In our pursuit of whom

We love.

Time Began With the Presence

Time began with the presence

Of God entering this world

And man made in God's image

By his presence entered time

Which is not day and night

But the presence of one who

Sees both in light and darkness.

The only fear

God had for man

Was that only light

Or darkness

Would be seen;

His only hope that

Knowing both would mean more

Than knowing just one

Otherwise no seamless robe

To be made that holds the

Day and night equally.

Your Presence Is Never
Your presence is never

Far

      And that is what

Our hope comes

        From.

We follow the incense of your

Presence,

The shadow of your body

Into places we'd never go

And find we've been lead

Into another part

Of who we are we would

Have never discovered.

Our love for the one we love

Is close to Your presence

That draws us to and through and beyond

But even though that takes us far

It does not take us as far

As You do.

      After awhile,

If we follow you,

           We cannot

Get rid of the incense in our nostrils

Taking us into whom

We are

      But would never be without You.

The One Who Works Against You
The one who works against you

From inside is

        Your brother,

Your sister

        One who you know intimately

Though pretend ignorance

So much, you think, unlike you

How could a relative like that exist?

Sometimes the battle cries

Freezes your blood, halts your desire

But what unnerves you most

Is the silence

        You

Understand and know

And embrace.

Wherever I Go, There's God

Wherever I go, there's God:

I make love with Michele,

There God is,

Naked, moaning, sweating

With us.

I speak with our children,

God leans in to hear.

I hunt, I work, I read, I write –

I'm never alone.

It took me

A long time to get used

To that,

Now I don't

Mind.

Sometimes God reminds me

So much of myself I

Get confused

Then hear

That infectious divine laughter

That makes me laugh too.

Whatever I Do When the Heart

Whatever I do when the heart

Is looking through the eyes

I do with You.

The only time I really

Lose You is when

My mind lectures me on its nature

Of seeing things.

Then my heart rebels and runs in Your direction.

You're easy to find

And when I'm with You

I am more of whom I am.

I like it best, though,

When I act and see as though

I have never to remember one moment

Of You being with me.

I Have Learned and Still Am Taught

I have learned, and still am taught,

That when I move in fear

What is sought is never caught;

And without the fear I seek nothing

And everything comes to me

That I need, desire, want.

I don't always

Do this well,

But when I do, I know exactly

Where "the kingdom of heaven is among you" is.

After You Repeat After Me

After you repeat after Me,

I am

      Then you need to

Go and become

In whatever form fills you out:

I have no plans like that for you,

Only that when you are who you are to be.

When I am becomes you,

Then I'm with you in whatever

You do

The way I

Have always been with those

Who learn to know my voice

Whispering, "Come to Me"

In every age,

In every age,

In every age

          Eternally.

So Many Things Have Been

So many things have been

Said about You in the same

Way for so long

        It's hard

To listen.

That's why I speak of You,

Of You in me,

In tree, cloud, animal,

In the blind, in the lame

In full and emptied desires,

In everything and everyone

So close your shadow shadows

Ours.

        That's enough, though,

To turn our eyes, our ears, our hearts

Towards new words that some won't speak

Because they never see the shadows.

We Are Born With the Voice of God

We are born with the voice of God

In our hearts.

    What He says is,

"Go on depart. I just won't look

The same when you see

Me there.

    There's beauty and terror

There; they each have something to give

You can't get from anything else –

                Take it.

Squeeze My hand one last time

So you'll know it is

Mine guiding your from time to time."

I Have Given You Metaphor
I have given you metaphor

To understand the world,

Your life, and Me clearly.

All facts support the metaphorical

Insights first seen, first known.

That is the second proposition

To the first that is I am.

When arguments are built to support

Me, walk away –

        Your eyes

Will tell you

        What your heart

Knows, has known, and will always

Know about you and Me.

Before Any Scripture Written

Before any scripture written

There was the earth speaking

In its dark, moist

Yielding, strengthening language

That every man and woman

Listening could understand.

Sometimes I think

The whole resurrection story

Was because God watched the earth

And saw something so clear

That all of creation

Became metaphor for what God's eyes saw,

God's heart heard

So even if all language was forgotten

The earth's scripture would remain.

No Mistake
No mistake:

What He seeks from us

Is what we seek from

Him

        To see if when after

Winter snows,

After spring seductions,

After the lushness and lust of summer,

After the beauty and nakedness of fall

We have the strength,

The deep allure to survive

In this world, other world

Grace we seek from him

He seeks in us.

        If we do, we see

Him as He is to be seen by each

One of us; if not, He seeks

Brushing aside the scattered leaves and debris

We have become.

I Am What You Are Not

I am what you are not,

              Yet that part of me

That is You keeps me

Finding You in all I do,

Wherever I look, whatever I touch,

Whatever I taste and smell and hear

You are always near in some form,

Some sense I cannot, do not escape

And my freedom is losing myself

To find You

      So I can be found

Again in everyone, everything

Seamlessly the robe covering and revealing

At just the right time, at just the right time.

I Am Not Afraid Of the Dark

I am not afraid of the dark

But there is something in me

That makes me fearful;

               Although

I am generally drawn to You

Through desire and love,

               Sometimes

I am pushed by this fear to find

You and always this fear never lets

Me find anything

           So some shaman

Appears who does not know what

I fear but knows fear and

The strength it can give and reminds

Me how to resurrect that.

               If

You are in everything, where are

You in this fear?

How do we

Find each other there?

This I am truly alone in

And can only utter the final

Prayer of freedom and hope –

"My God! Why have you forsaken me?"

So I See You

So I see You

      And having done so

Love You.

      Sometimes that love has

Stifled me like some siren song

Calls to my love and destruction;

But I have awaken because

I did not hear your deep, silent

Voice in those songs.

      Your love

Makes me unlike others –

      I have been

Taught, by You, to bear the joys and sorrows.

Your Son taught You that –

      Sometimes I

Get confused whose teaching me.

      Never mind:

Like all sons, His shoulders

Carry more than his father's

And I am Your son too.

How I Have Known You

How I have known You

I no longer do

    As what I

Come to know about myself changes

Where and how I see You.

Some would call this a falling away:

I call it a falling towards

Where I leap into the vast ignorance of each day

And something new is given

So I can practice the right

Kind of forgetfulness so each

Moment appears complete, new

And You and I are fully there

Like we have never been before.

The Drama of Our Lives
The drama of our lives

Invites the One

Into our lives.

It's a known, open

Invitation.

    We don't always

See that One entering;

We never know this One

Is around

    Until

        After the fact

And that sense of is

Enters everything;

    Sometimes

We catch ourselves being

Who we truly are as if surprised –

That's a sign, too, that One is around.

There's nothing wrong with drama—

That is our life,

Once Jacob, At Five Said

Once Jacob, at five said,

"Everyone makes God

After their own image"

So God and Jesus

And the story always

Gets retold in its

Own way

        Ad infinitum

Eternally making

The sense it is finally.

What We Take In We Put Back

What we take in we put back

Out piecemeal, patch-worked

Into a moment of wholeness

                While You

Never see anything partially

But whole

       Past present future

And sometimes we see like that

Because we are part of one another

But just can't say when or how

We see that way,

           The way

You always do.

You Are the Shape-shifter

You are the Shape-shifter,

The One always found

Anywhere at any time,

The unexpected moment,

        The expected.

We are Sirens calling to You

To stay put

        Because we like to

Catch and not release

        But You

Turn suddenly into the divinity

You are

Calling us to change with You. . . .

It Is Difficult

To lead the life you are to lead.

So many want the life

They never lived

        Lived through You.

And we, being creatures who like to please,

Often, sometimes almost always,

Lose ourselves in the wrong way

Until we realize how

Lost we are –

        Our words sound strange,

Our bodies look unfamiliar,

Memories seem to belong to someone

Else

        And suddenly we

Find our voice, our acts, our bodies,

Our stories

        And we are who we

Are finally

    Following and leading

The life that is ours. . .

                Or not –

Every story doesn't end the way

It wants to.

The First Falsehood

The first falsehood

We learn is that we

Struggle against outside

Forces –

    Not true:

We struggle against ourselves

But early lose the faith

A maple seed inherently

Possesses.

    Still, we

See nature and something

Inside says, Yes

        To that

Living promise that is

Everywhere singing

Its song to us

To join our voice to

Its thousand,

Thousand

Voices we hear

                          Endless

That we first heard in a pause

Of silence that was our first

Ripening.

I Am Asked
How do you know?

How do you not?

I reply.

Every wrestler I face

Has some divine grace

That cuts a muscle deeper.

It's always that way;

I attack You;

You attack me

    And the victory

Is mutual.

    That's how it

Is between loving

Opponents who need

One another

    To show

The strength that comes

From each.

Where Our Freedom Lies

And where our freedom lies

Is inside us

        Where we

Come fully into view

Of ourselves and God.

              Oh yes, God;

We need to feel His eyes in

Ours so we can see, if just

For a moment, ourselves from

A divine point-of-view.

Where else does freedom reign

If not in the divinity that

Infuses blood and bone,

Heart and mind,

Word and act

And trusting, trusting

That we, like love,

Come to bear all things

Graciously as the treasure

They are.

In This Generation or the Next

In this generation or the next,

God is sought

    Because that urge

To be found, by us and God,

Can't stay hidden too long –

Sooner or later

One of us starts calling

To the other.

Who and What We

Who and what we

Love is You

               So

You may be accessible

To us in all and any degree

On the earth.

You are rain or sun,

Night or day.

There is no way for

You to not be in

What we need, desire,

Love.

       There You are

Waiting again for us

To embrace You.

All Has Been Lost

All has been lost

Because our rulers are bankers

And their sons accountants not

In the exchange of souls;

Their daughters caught in fashion,

Not beauty.

No wonder the world of men implodes

As Nature waits for their return

To the natural nobility

Breathed into each of them

The way Adam was given life

Long ago.

And When We Come Again

Risen from our crucifixion

Listening to the love talk of Jesus

Multiplying one and one to equal

That third who is the only One

And says we may be too

Through Him

Then all will be restored

And what has been weak will be

Strong,

And what has been divided will be

Unified,

And no church nor any theology

Will imprison God for us anymore

And at evening we'll all have

Our walk with God

As it was in the beginning.

We Are Not Weak
We are not weak

When we find who we are

Covering the muscles we developed

To fight in this world that are useless.

Our strength will come

From everything

We are in which leaves

Nothing vacant.

We draw upon You in all time,

From all places

We seek You, You seek us

In silence and solitude

To walk abroad in Your strength

Of grace--

    You in everyone, everything

Drawing us to You.

This Quest Goes On, Is Handed Off

This quest goes on, is handed off

With each one who leaves this life,

They leave their desire

                          To continue

To find the Divine fleshed out,

The lips of God a recent memory

With the first breath of life breathed in.

It just does not stop.

Even those who say they have nothing of

You in them surprise themselves

And others every day by serendipitous

Acts of grace unexplainable,

Unreasoned, unthought-of but there

Just the same.

Everyone seeks the holy name

They are to hear – no-one

Has any confusion about that.

Always For

I always look for

You seeing the beauty

Of Your divine presence shadowed

In everywhere I cast my eyes.

The beauty of this world is

Only complete when seen through

Your eyes, touched by your hands, heard by your ears,

Tasted by Your mouth

That sometimes suddenly becomes mine.

Always I am looking for Christ

 "That spittle and mud on my eyes again, please"

And more often than not my sight

Is restored.

There Is No Denying How Far Away

There is no denying how far away

Everything feels the more

I spin the web of words

That cannot hold anything.

When I seek what is not mine,

Everything grows hard --

                My touch

Becomes Midas metalling

Everyone, all my acts through the slightest

Touch of me.

       Still, there is Your

Whisper that comes to me

With the slight shrug of the shoulders

And raised eyebrows and closed lip smile

Saying, "See?"

           I nod, agree and slowly

I start to drop things that have

Kept me from dancing with You

Saying, "Would You like to lead?"

And You reply, as my heart is

Taken again, "We'll see."

"My Help Cometh from the Hills"

"My help cometh from the hills"

David wrote saying more about

God in six words than books

A thousand pages long.

When we dream, where do we dream

Our freedom if not in hills and valleys,

Rivers and lakes,

Blue sky, wild game

Our beloved by our side outside under an

Open sky.

    There's more of God

In a hillside than in any book.

In towns and cities there's just

Enough room to get by,

And no place of worship can hold

What nature, God's first handiwork, holds

For us to see

Simply there in complete eye-beholding majesty.

You Cannot Find God in Cities
You cannot find God in cities

Where streets are laid out in

Rectangular precision –

God blends into this then that

Without distinction or brick and mortar.

Children cannot find their souls,

The old offer no wisdom,

And those between are a blur,

A tick on the clock of deadlines

Meaningless.

      If you want God

Or yourself, there has, at least,

To be a path to some spot of

Nature that says, "Take off

Your shoes – you're on holy ground."

If We Cannot Pray

If we cannot pray

For our deaths,

How can we pray

For our life?

Help us to do so

And let all that which

Would keep us from living

Fall away the way leaves

Fall, decay, then turn up

Green again.

    We want to live;

Help us to die so we may do so –

Passion, crucifixion, resurrection

As natural as breathing –

Inhale, exhale, alive.

Deepest Desire

Our deepest desire is to die

So we can live freely

Moving unselfconsciously

In gracious word and act naturally

In every moment we are.

Everything in us moves in that

Leaf falling direction to come up

Green at each spring that knows only

Its own growth

        Except for

That part of us that will not water

Anything—

          If we can get through that

Then we can sing our deaths joyfully

To be alive.

Our Greatest Fear

Our greatest fear is that we will

Not live before we die the deaths,

Yes deaths necessary for life.

We know that is what we are to do,

But fear that word death so much

We don't die willingly to live freely

As who we are.

                       There is something that

Pulls us and keeps us from going

Far enough into, then through

The darkness that is the promise

And fulfillment of light.

Help us, oh God, to die

So we might live as You have taught us

In everything we see and do.

The Proclamation of Who I Am

The proclamation of who I am

Is always in ready

To prepare the way as soon

As I utter those divine words

Whispered in my ears by God:

"I am that I am."

When that happens, the rocks and sky

Cry in incantations long remembered

So old now new

And I walk everywhere

Unprepared, waiting for the whatever

That moment is ready to give.

I Want To Hear Your Voice

I want to hear Your voice

Wherever I am but especially

When fear starts to move me

Let me hear Your words

So the fear disappears and I

Stand on holy ground because

You have to spoken to me and I have heard and that is

Enough for me to act out

Of whom I am, they way

You are

    Completely, totally present

At every when in every now.

What Is True Is How I Can Be

What is true is how I can be

Close to You, to You --

Nothing else.

If this act, this fact

Of all life was drawn in

Like the breath it is,

We would all be who

We are to be naturally.

And The Seduction of What

And the seduction of what

Has been good, bad, indifferent

Has a strong grip on what is

And what is to come though

Secretly longs to be set

Free of holding

What deserves no hands.

Everything in Nature

Turns into this freedom

Of using what has been given

Into what does not harden

Into brick and cement

That eventually crumbles

To the freedom of dust

Collected again, shaped, created

Breathed into life willing

To let go.

The Wealth That Matters
The wealth that matters

Sits on the carpet woven

By intimacy that does not

Fear anyone, anything

And is beyond the value of how

We place value here, there.

It draws the treasure of those

Who are true;

           They enter,

Naked and nothing clothes

Them better.

      These are like

Pearls on a necklace –

The string of their wealth holds

Them together though they've been

Collected far from one another.

If you want that wealth,

Stop hiding your self

From your self –

        Nothing matters but this

Wealth that can't be worn but only known.

We Who Lack the Riches of the World

We who lack the riches of the world

Do not lack ourselves

As we wonder wondering why

We are not like others

Who seem to be able to cling, to grasp

To and after what our hands cannot hold.

We are the earth's

Growing in storm and sun,

Hot and cold

Deeply we root down

To rise up

As every creature, every plant, every

Body of water, every piece of land

Just is who it is

Sufficient in its interdependence on every –

Everything, everyone, every moment.

When You Have Given Up the Quest
When you have given up the quest for

Yourself, you are the beggar at every

Turn, the wolf that hasn't eaten

For days,

    The one who refuses to ask

The question of freedom because

Freedom is always about serving the right

Master not doing what you think

Satisfies your desires born out of remembering

And dead emotion cohabiting for destruction.

Even then in the sleeplessness of

Your night dream flicks a hope that

Wakes you for a second

    To see if you will

Decide to pursue hope or to stay in the world of fear.

Everywhere You Step

Everywhere you step,

The earth says,

"Plant a little root

Of yourself here to feel

The sun, the overcast sky,

The snow, the rain. Leave

A piece of yourself everywhere

The way I do adding

Grace and beauty by being

Simply where you are if only

For a moment or two

Completely."

The Voice of God Is Like the Wind

The voice of God is like the wind

That starts and stops

Bending trees, moving fallen

Leaves, carrying song and incense

Here then there.

                When the wind blows,

Nothing tries to ignore it;

So with God's voice to the listening

Soul ready to go, to stop

In every moment just so

                      Complete.

The Trees Know Nothing of the Laws

The trees know nothing of the laws

Of Nature so caught up in going down

And coming up.

                So those whose hearts

Break all laws to live free and whole

Have this in common with all Nature –

Survive, thrive

Give beauty, inspire grace

Receive courage and let love bear

All things to each end lovingly, always lovingly.

Yes

It's true: there's little that can be

Forgiven in cities everything is so

Straight and cornered, measured, time

Doled out in shifts, feet touching concrete.

It doesn't take much:

A dream of some horizon,

At the edge of the city a glimpse of the land beyond,

Even a park appearing out of nowhere

And something inside sighs deep relief

And hope in the fact of a grace that cannot

Be denied.

It Has Taken Me a Long Time

It has taken me a long time

(And still at times I forget)

That everyone, everything

Teaches me something especially

Those I love recklessly

In utter abandon

                      Until

Even the softest whisper

Guides me, one word opens

Me to the force that flows

Through everything through me

Keeping me where I am

As I am

Uttering, chanting

I am that I am

Kicking my sandals off

Again.

Made in the USA
Middletown, DE
10 December 2021